Word Bird's

Dinosaur Days

Published in the United States of America by The Child's World®, Inc.
PO Box 326
Chanhassen, MN 55317-0326
800-599-READ
www.childsworld.com

Project Manager Mary Berendes
Editor Katherine Stevenson, Ph.D.
Designer Ian Butterworth

Library of Congress Cataloging-in-Publication Data
Moncure, Jane Belk.
Word Bird's dinosaur days / by Jane Belk Moncure.
p. cm.
Summary: After a trip to the museum, Word Bird and
his classmates have a "Dinosaur Day" at school.
ISBN 1-56766-999-9 (lib. : alk. paper)
[1. Dinosaurs—Fiction. 2. School field trips—Fiction.
3. Schools—Fiction. 4. Birds—Fiction. 5. Animals—Fiction.] I. Title.
PZ7.M739 Wof 2002
[E]—dc21
2001006056

Word Bird's™

Dinosaur Days

by Jane Belk Moncure

illustrated by Chris McEwan

TYRANNOSAURUS

"We are off to see the dinosaurs,"
sang Word Bird and all the other
friends. Their big yellow bus went
down the road to the museum.

It was a special day at the museum—
Dinosaur Day!
"Here we are," said their teacher,
Miss Beary. "Everyone follow me."

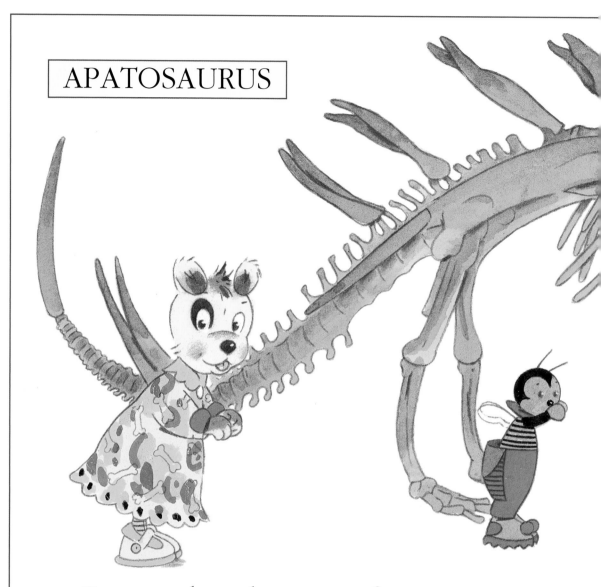

APATOSAURUS

Guess what they saw first?
Lots of dinosaur bones!
"I like those big bones," said Dog.
"I don't," said Bee. "I think
dinosaurs are scary."

"They can't hurt you," said Word Bird.
"They are dead."
"We can learn what they looked like
  when they were alive," said Miss Beary.
"Let's go look at some dinosaur models."

TYRANNOSAURUS

First they saw a model of a big
dinosaur with sharp teeth. Bee
hid behind Word Bird.
"Don't worry," said Word Bird.
"It's not real."

STEGOSAURUS

Next they saw a dinosaur
with spikes on its back.
"I would not like to ride on
that dinosaur," said Dog.

DIPLODOCUS

Then they saw a dinosaur with a
long neck and a very long tail.

"We could all ride on that tail," said Cat.
"Not me," said Bee.

TRICERATOPS

"How about riding on this one?"
asked Word Bird. "I would like
to ride on a dinosaur. That
would be fun."

"Well, I have a surprise for you,"
said Miss Beary. "It's in the park
across the street."

Guess what? Word Bird did ride a
dinosaur. Did everyone climb up
on the dinosaur's back?

No! Not Bee! Bee just watched.
"I do not like dinosaurs," Bee said.

We went to the museum. We saw dinosaurs. We rode on a dinosaur, too. We had fun.

The next day, Miss Beary said, "Let's have our own Dinosaur Day here at school."
First the class wrote a story about their trip.

Then they went to the library to find
other stories about dinosaurs. Word
Bird found a really big book.
"I will read my book to Papa tonight,"
Word Bird said.

At lunchtime there were carrots in
Word Bird's lunch box.
"Guess what I have for lunch?"
Word Bird asked.
"Carrots," said Bunny.

"No," said Word Bird. "They are orange
   dinosaur teeth. We can each have one."
"No, thank you," said Bee.

After lunch the class painted pictures.
Bunny painted a big dinosaur with
sharp teeth. Cat painted a dinosaur
with a long tail.

Word Bird painted a dinosaur with horns.
But Bee painted a tree.

At music time, the class sang a
funny dinosaur song. Then they
did a funny dinosaur dance.

If I were a dinosaur,
I would be as long as a bus
And as tall as a tree.
When I went for a walk,
This is how it would be—
Thump! Thump! Thump! Thump!

As they danced, they stomped their feet. Thump! Thump! Thump! What did Bee do?

After school, Bee and Dog
came to play with Word Bird.
"Let's dig for dinosaur bones,"
said Dog.
"Good idea," said Word Bird.

After a while, Bee said,
"I can ride a dinosaur all by myself."
Word Bird and Dog jumped off.
Bee rode alone. Then Word Bird said,
"Let's go play with my dinosaurs."

"We can have dinosaur races,"
said Dog. Bee chose the biggest
dinosaur of all.
"I think I will win," Bee said.
And Bee did.

That night, Word Bird read the
big dinosaur book to Papa.
"Dog and I like dinosaurs," Word
Bird said. "Now Bee likes them,
too. This has been the best
Dinosaur Day of all!"

Can you read these dinosaur names with Word Bird?

Apatosaurus
(uh-pah-tuh-SOR-us)

Tyrannosaurus
(tih-ra-nuh-SOR-us)

Stegosaurus
(ste-guh-SOR-us)

Triceratops
(try-SAYR-uh-tops)

Diplodocus
(dih-PLAH-duh-kus)